DATE DUE

FAMOUS FIGURES OF

ANNIE OAKLEY

THE AMERICAN FRONTIER

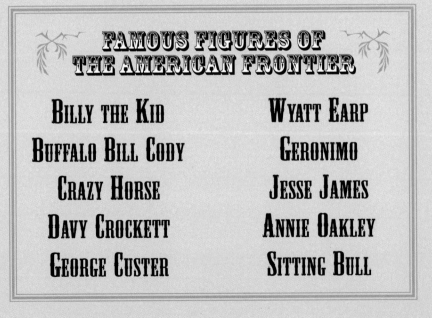

FAMOUS FIGURES OF THE AMERICAN FRONTIER

BILLY THE KID

BUFFALO BILL CODY

CRAZY HORSE

DAVY CROCKETT

GEORGE CUSTER

WYATT EARP

GERONIMO

JESSE JAMES

ANNIE OAKLEY

SITTING BULL

FAMOUS FIGURES OF

ANNIE OAKLEY

THE AMERICAN FRONTIER

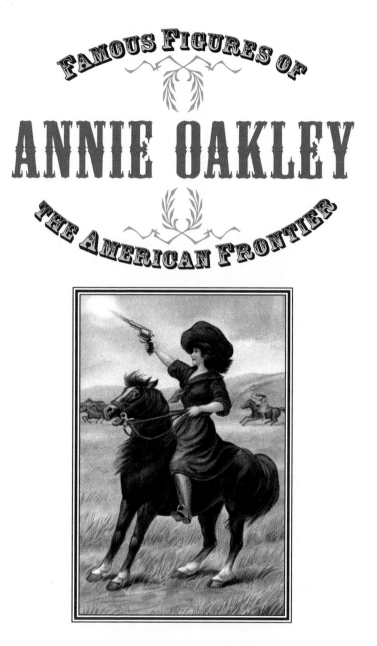

CHARLES J. SHIELDS

CHELSEA HOUSE PUBLISHERS
PHILADELPHIA

Produced for Chelsea House by
OTTN Publishing, Stockton, NJ

CHELSEA HOUSE PUBLISHERS
Editor in Chief: Sally Cheney
Associate Editor in Chief: Kim Shinners
Production Manager: Pamela Loos
Art Director: Sara Davis
Series Designer: Keith Trego

First Printing

1 3 5 7 9 8 6 4 2

The Chelsea House World Wide Web address is
http://www.chelseahouse.com

Library of Congress Cataloging-in-Publication Data

Shields, Charles J.
Annie Oakley / by Charles J. Shields.
    p.   cm. – (Famous figures of the American frontier)
Includes bibliographical references and index.
    ISBN 0-7910-6489-1 (alk. paper)
    ISBN 0-7910-6490-5 (pbk.: alk. paper)
1. Oakley, Annie, 1860-1926–Juvenile literature. 2. Shooters
of firearms–United States–Biography–Juvenile literature.
3. Women entertainers–United States–Biography–Juvenile
literature. [1. Oakley, Annie, 1860-1926. 2. Sharpshooters.
3. Entertainers. 4. Women–Biography] I. Title. II. Series.

GV1157.O3 S55 2001
799.3'092–dc21   2001028866

CONTENTS

Barry
Photo

Annie Oakley poses with her gun in this 1887 photograph. She had already built a career as a trick shot when she was invited to join Buffalo Bill's Wild West Show. The show would launch her to incredible popularity both in the United States and in Europe.

AN AMERICAN LEGEND

Nate Salsbury had seen pretty much everything in show business. He had been a respected actor and later the manager of a highly successful touring company called the Troubadours. Hundreds of entertainers had *auditioned* for him—some good, many poor.

So when Buffalo Bill Cody—the Pony Express rider and army scout turned showman—asked Salsbury to help him manage a whole new concept in entertainment called the Wild West Show, Salsbury signed on. He could see the appeal of such a spectacle. Folks would be treated to a whirling *kaleidoscope* of Indians in war dress, deafening pistol shoot-outs, hard-riding cowboys, thrilling ambushes, and even reenactments of historic incidents, such as Custer's

An 1899 poster for Buffalo Bill's Wild West Show. After meeting the show's manager, Nate Salsbury, Annie Oakley joined the show in 1885. The female sharpshooter soon became one of the Wild West Show's favorite attractions.

defeat at the Little Bighorn. It would be part circus, part theater, and part American history lesson.

Unfortunately, though, a short time after its *debut* in Omaha, Nebraska, the Wild West Show struck a vein of bad luck. In December 1884, a steamship carrying some of the show's equipment down the Mississippi River collided with another steamer and sank. Cody's partner, Captain Adam H. Bogardus, a popular sharpshooter whose demonstrations of *marksmanship* filled grandstands with audiences, lost his guns, targets, and props in the

accident. Disgusted, Bogardus went with his three sons to recover damages from the steamship company. Afterward, he decided to pull out of his partnership with Cody altogether.

In April 1885, the Wild West Show, deeply in debt, was camped in St. Louis. On the morning of the 24th, Salsbury was strolling among the white tents when something drew his attention. Down in the arena, a young couple was setting up to audition, and Salsbury–always on the lookout for talent–took a seat in the **grandstands** to watch. The woman was small, only about five feet tall, with dark, flowing hair. Salsbury was surprised when she produced a rack of shotguns and loaded them. She looked too small to withstand the hard punch in the shoulder from a shotgun's **recoil**. The man helping her was strong looking, though, and he seemed a more likely candidate to be handling a shotgun.

Suddenly, the arena was alive with gunfire. The man threw glass balls high into the air, and the woman shattered them rapidly. She fired from her right side, from her left–and even held the shotgun upside down and blasted away. For a moment, there was a pause while the man set up a mechanical device and she chose another shotgun. Then she shouted, "Pull!" and a clay pigeon went sailing out across the arena like a bird. She fired and pulverized the target into a puff of gray dust.

Salsbury had seen enough. He hurried down the grandstand steps. "Fine! Wonderful!" he exclaimed. "Have you got some photographs with your gun?" He didn't even know the woman's name, but he was already thinking of ways to publicize her.

Her name was Annie Oakley, and the man with her was her husband and business manager, Frank Butler. Only 10 years before, she had lived in an orphanage because her mother was destitute. She and Butler had met in a shooting contest after she had learned to hunt for a living. In the few years following their marriage, she had perfected a trick shooting act. But her *winsome* personality was what captivated audiences most.

Nate Salsbury was not immune to her charm, either. He hired her on the spot, without even consulting Buffalo Bill. He knew outstanding talent when he saw it.

And he was right. Not only would Annie Oakley become one of the main attractions of the Wild West Show, but over the years she would become something even more rare–a genuine American legend.

"There's a charming little girl / She's many miles from here / She's a loving little fairy / You'd fall in love to see her," Frank Butler, a champion marksman, wrote in a poem about Annie. Frank and Annie would marry after she defeated him in a shooting contest.

A Charming Little Girl

The girl who would gain fame as Annie Oakley was born Phoebe Ann Moses (or Mauzy, according to the U.S. census of 1860) to a Quaker couple in a log cabin in Darke County, Ohio, on August 13, 1860. Her parents, Jacob and Susan Moses, arrived in the northeastern corner of the county in the 1850s. They were making a fresh start after their tavern in Hollidaysburg,

Pennsylvania, burned down. Their new home was nicknamed "the wilds," because the land had been virgin forest only a few years earlier.

Phoebe Ann was the youngest of five daughters. Her sisters didn't like the name Phoebe, so they called her Annie instead. The sisters also had a brother who was two years younger than Annie.

Disaster struck the Moses family in 1866 when Annie was six. One winter day, Jacob set out with a wagonload of grain for the local mill 14 miles away. As the family expected, he was gone all day, but then a blizzard struck. Finally, sometime around midnight, Susan and the children heard the creak of wagon wheels outside the cabin. "Mother threw the door wide open into the face of the howling wind," Annie recalled years later. There was her father, the reins wrapped around his wrists and neck, trying to stay upright in the wagon seat. His hands were frozen and he could not speak. After the storm a doctor came, but there was little he could do. Despite months of bed rest, Jacob died that spring, probably from *pneumonia*.

More calamities followed. The fatherless family had trouble paying the bills. Then Annie's eldest sister died. To pay for the funeral, Annie's mother sold their only cow. With poverty facing them, Mrs. Moses was forced to take painful and drastic steps. She sent one daughter to live with another family– and she placed Annie, age 10, at the county *poor farm*, a shelter for orphans and homeless persons.

To take a resident away from the poor farm, off the county's hands, was considered a kindness. So when a farmer came looking for a girl to serve as a companion to his wife and baby, Annie went with him. She never gave the real name of this family in her *autobiography*, but she called them "the Wolves." They made her into their slave.

"I got up at 4:00 in the morning," she wrote later, "got breakfast, milked the cows, washed dishes, skimmed milk, fed the cows and pigs, pumped water for the cattle, fed the chickens, rocked the baby to sleep, weeded the garden, picked wild blueberries and got dinner." The Wolves beat her when she failed to do her work to their liking, leaving scars and permanent welts on her back. At last she could take no more; she ran away, back to the poor farm, where she stayed for another two years. Then she returned home to her mother.

Annie was now about 15. Her mother had remarried, been widowed again, and gotten married

Annie had first fired a gun when she was eight. "I saw a squirrel run down over the grass in front of the house, through the orchard and stop on a fence to get a hickory nut," she remembered. She hurried into the cabin, climbed on a chair, and took down her father's rifle from the mantel above the fireplace. Lugging it back outside, she propped the barrel of the rifle on the porch railing and took aim. Her shot hit home and killed the squirrel.

a third time. Her new stepfather welcomed Annie, but the family was in tough straits and close to losing their farm. Annie decided she could help by hunting food for her family—and selling the leftovers to others.

A pair of brothers owned a store in nearby Greenville that sold game animals such as quail, pheasant, rabbit, deer, and turkey to the kitchens of hotels in Cincinnati. Annie approached the brothers with an offer: she would furnish as much game as they could sell. They struck a deal, and Annie was in business as a "market hunter."

The petite, dark-haired girl, dressed in heavy cotton work clothes and carrying her father's old-fashioned muzzle-loading rifle, became a familiar sight in town. Annie brought in a staggering amount of game—150 to 200 white-tailed deer in a single autumn, for instance. The Cincinnati hotels purchased her meat as fast as she provided it. Soon Annie was making more money than most men, and she was able to pay the entire *mortgage* on her mother and stepfather's farm.

By the time she was in her late teens, Annie's reputation as a deadeye shot became so well known that she was barred from local shooting contests. It was not fair to let her compete. Meanwhile, a young man named Frank Butler had already discovered that shooting contests and performances paid pretty well, if you were a crack shot.

Butler was born in Ireland. After he *emigrated,* sailing to America, he scraped by as best he could–selling newspapers in New York City, cleaning stables, loading and unloading milk wagons, and even begging when he had to. For two years he worked on a fishing boat, and he married and had two children. That marriage fizzled and ended in divorce.

By nature, Frank was an outgoing and humorous man, so he drifted into *vaudeville.* Vaudeville was a type of theater entertainment in the mid-19th to the mid-20th centuries that featured a variety of acts–acrobats, magicians, singers, dancers, comedians, and other performers. Butler entered the spotlight with a trained dog act. Then he discovered that trick shooting was more in demand, so he taught himself that skill. He learned to hit fixed targets while leaning over backward or by aiming in a mirror. Exhibitions of hitting targets hurled into the air drew crowds, too.

Butler worked with two partners—a man named Baughman and a trained poodle named George. They performed first in vaudeville and then with the Sells Brothers' Circus. In April 1881, they were in Cincinnati, ready to rejoin the circus in Cleveland for another season, when a farmer in their hotel bet $100 that he knew someone who could outshoot Butler. "I thought there were some country people who thought someone could shoot a little and were ready to lose money," Butler said later, "and as I needed it, I went out."

When Butler finally arrived at the remote spot, known as Shooter's Hill, to his surprise he found hundreds of people waiting. He was further amazed when his opponent turned out to be a polite young woman named Annie Moses. Butler tipped his hat and said it was a pleasure to meet her.

Their contest consisted of shooting at circular clay targets, called pigeons, flung into the air by a

A colorful poster advertises the Sells Brothers' Circus. Frank Butler was a sharpshooter with the circus, waiting for the season to begin, when he accepted a bet that would change his life—a shooting match against a local girl. Butler was just four years older than Annie Moses when the match took place.

machine called a trap. The formal setting of the contest and the clay pigeons were strange to Annie— but she defeated Frank, hitting 23 of a possible 25 targets, to 21 by Butler. All her life, Annie remembered the view from Shooter's Hill, the cheers from the admiring audience, and her excitement at going toe-to-toe with the handsome and **intriguing** man standing beside her.

The contest was Butler's first loss, and he too was intrigued. A stream of correspondence followed between Annie and Butler. Their correspondence grew more and more affectionate. A year after the shooting contest, they were married.

Annie takes careful aim in a mirror during a trick shot. Annie filled in for her husband's partner during one of their shows and proved to be a crowd-pleaser. Frank taught her many tricks, and she soon launched her own career as a markswoman.

FRANK AND ANNIE

Frank Butler and his wife Annie kept a watchful eye on their finances while they took work as professional sharpshooters as often as they could. Show business is filled with stories of famous personalities who made and lost a fortune. Perhaps because they had been poor as children, the Butlers, on the other hand, managed their public lives like a family business.

Not long after they were married in June 1882, Annie went to stay with friends in Erie, Pennsylvania—or perhaps to attend school there, some sources say—because Frank was going on the road with a new partner, John Graham. Graham and Butler billed themselves as "champion all-around shots" and went in for fancy shooting. They sat on chairs a few yards apart and shot an apple off each other's head. Butler did his bend-over-backward trick; Graham dropped his head down to his knees and fired between his legs.

One night Graham was too ill to perform, but Annie happened to be present. She stepped in as Frank's assistant. During one part of the show, Frank was supposed to hit a difficult target. He usually pretended to miss a few times, just to make the performance more dramatic, but on this night, with Annie looking on, he couldn't hit the target at all.

A man in the crowd shouted, "Let the girl shoot!"

Annie had never tried the trick, but on the second shot, she hit the target. Frank tried to get back in the act, but the audience was in an uproar. "Let the girl shoot!" they insisted. Annie finished the show, and in the process launched her own career as an audience-pleasing trick shot.

The tools of a shooter's trade: a shotgun, broken open for loading; shotgun shells, which contain powder and small metal balls, or "shot"; and round orange clay targets, called "pigeons." When these small clay pigeons are launched into the sky, using a machine called a trap, the shooter has just a few moments to aim and fire.

About this time she took her stage name, Annie Oakley (although in private she continued to introduce herself as Mrs. Butler). How she chose "Oakley" isn't clear. Some sources say it was the name of a Cincinnati suburb. Others insist she simply liked the sound of the name. In any case, she and Frank quickly established a professional personality for Annie Oakley that was a good fit with her values.

First, she would not cheat like some "champion shots" who deceived their audiences. Pistols could be doctored to shoot **buckshot**, for example, so that hitting targets was easier. Another trick involved placing a candle in front of a small wooden block; the concussion of a bullet hitting the block anywhere within three inches of the flame extinguished it, making it appear that it had been snuffed out by the bullet itself. The cigarette trick was another piece of fakery. Audiences gasped when a shooter clipped the ashes off a burning cigarette held between the lips of an assistant—but actually, a tiny wire ran through the center of the cigarette, which the assistant flicked hard at just the right instant, making the ashes fly off. Annie Oakley scorned all of these tricks. She never relied on anything except her skill.

Second, she was modest in her appearance and behavior. She saw no contradiction in being a crack shot who also happened to be a lady. When the audi-

Many female circus performers wore tights to add sex appeal to their act—but Annie would have none of that. She designed, sewed, and embroidered her own costumes. They were usually a kind of riding outfit: long skirt, tight long-sleeved jacket or blouse, and leggings.

ence applauded a trick, she beamed a radiant smile and curtsied demurely. At the end of her act, she ran off lightly with a little skip. The contrast between her remarkable ability with firearms and her feminine behavior increased her popularity. Newspapers often described her performance as "delightful" or "captivating."

Once the Butlers realized that Annie could be a bigger attraction than Frank, he started teaching her all the tricks he had mastered. She practiced with him until she could shoot a dime tossed in the air, snuff out flames on a rotating wheel, and perform half a dozen other crowd-pleasers. She was so good, Frank liked to boast with a twinkle in his eye, that she could scramble eggs in midair.

Soon after Annie's debut on the stage, probably in early 1883, they set out on the road together as a husband-and-wife act, playing vaudeville theaters and skating rinks. Annie passed over these days in her autobiography rather quickly, perhaps because the life of small-time performers was not especially interesting or glamorous. One or two big trunks held most of their belongings, which they lugged into inexpensive hotels and boardinghouses across a dozen states. During the day they practiced; at night they performed. On weekends, they often added an extra afternoon performance. They were by no means a sensation in show business, but in March 1884, Annie's career received a boost from someone famous—or *notorious*, depending whom you asked: the Sioux chief Sitting Bull.

Only eight years before, Sitting Bull had ordered the counterattack on Lieutenant Colonel George Armstrong Custer's Seventh Cavalry regiment at the Little Bighorn River in the Montana territory. During a ferocious, one-hour fight, 2,000 Sioux and

CHIEF SITTING BULL
SIOUX -

Sitting Bull was an important chief and medicine man of the Hunkpapa Sioux. For many years he led the Sioux in their fight to prevent the white settlement of Indian lands. He was impressed when he saw Annie shoot in the spring of 1884, and he nicknamed her "Little Sure Shot." This portrait of Sitting Bull was painted the next year, when Sitting Bull joined the Wild West Show.

Cheyenne warriors slaughtered Custer and more than 200 soldiers. Since then, the federal government had pursued a relentless policy of forcing all tribes onto **reservations**. But despite the humiliation, an air of authority and dignity clung to Sitting Bull. He accepted invitations from politicians and business leaders to view the achievements of white civilization, wisely understanding that he could serve as a representative of American Indians, who were largely powerless.

In March 1884, he was in St. Paul, Minnesota, being treated to a grand tour by city leaders. He visited a cigar factory and puffed appreciatively on a hand-rolled sample. He dropped in on the offices of the local newspaper and listened to voices on a telephone. "Waukon," he commented, the Sioux word for "the devil." One of his favorite stops was a public elementary school; there he visited classes and nodded delightedly when the fire alarm rang and all the children exited the building in a minute and 45 seconds.

On Wednesday night, March 19, he attended a performance at the Olympic Theater of the Arlington and Fields Combination, a standard variety show. He sat quietly watching the various performances–acrobatics, singing, and skits. Then the Butlers trotted onto the stage. Even before Annie had finished her *repertoire* of fancy shots, Sitting Bull was enchanted. After the show, he sent a messenger to her hotel, asking her to visit him. Annie, business-like as usual, apologized but said no. The chief would not be satisfied. He sent $65 with a request for her photograph. Taken aback, Annie would not accept the money but went to meet her sudden admirer the following morning.

Sitting Bull had lost a daughter during the Indian wars, and something about Annie must have touched his memories as a father. He expressed his fondness for her and announced that he would adopt her, conferring on her the name "Watanya Cicilla," or "Little Sure Shot." Annie saw no harm in the honor, and Frank saw an opportunity. He took out an ad in a show business publication, *The New York Clipper,* and headlined it "The Premier Shots, Butler and Oakley, Captured by Sitting Bull." The ad's description of the meeting added to the romance of Annie as a rootin'-tootin' western girl.

Neither Annie nor Frank knew it at the time, but Sitting Bull's name for her turned out to be more than just a little pleasantry. "Little Sure Shot" was an ideal nickname for Annie, and one day millions of Americans and Europeans would recognize her by that name.

Later that year, Annie and Frank joined the Sells Brothers' Circus. They were probably tired of making their own arrangements, and at least a circus would provide regular pay, lodgings, and play dates. But both of them were dismayed at the management's poor regard for safety, and they protested vigorously. Nevertheless, the Butlers met the terms of their contract and performed in 187 locations in 13 states during the season.

Then in mid-December, while they were playing the Sells Brothers' end-of-season shows in New Orleans, a newspaper story caught Frank's attention. Buffalo Bill Cody, creator of "Buffalo Bill's Wild West Show" was coming to town looking for talent. Frank realized in an instant that this could be just the big break he and Annie needed.

BUFFALO BILL'S WIL
AND CONGRESS OF ROUGH RIDERS OF

THE WILD WEST SHOW

A colorful poster advertises the Wild West Show, featuring Buffalo Bill on horseback at the right. Annie joined the show in the spring of 1885 and soon became a star.

uffalo Bill Cody's real name was William Frederick Cody. Born in 1846 in Iowa, he had been a Pony Express rider, Civil War soldier, trail scout, hunter, Indian fighter, and actor. He received his nickname because of his skill at buffalo hunting for the Kansas Pacific Railroad construction crews.

The idea for staging an outdoor show about the Old

Before starting the Wild West Show, Buffalo Bill Cody was already nationally famous. He had been a Pony Express rider and chief scout for the U.S. Army during the 1860s and 1870s. In addition, dozens of stories were published about his exploits—most of which were fictional.

West came to Buffalo Bill almost by accident. On a visit to North Platte, Nebraska, during the summer of 1882, Cody learned that the town had no official plans for the Fourth of July. He volunteered to organize a last-minute festival. Cody rounded up a stagecoach, some cowboys and Indians, and a small buffalo herd to stage exhibitions of western life. He also arranged for horse races and shooting contests.

Spectators from miles around descended on North Platte to see the show. Even though there were already nearly 50 circuses traveling the United States, the town had difficulty coping with crowds who wanted to see the "real West." Cody realized that the West had romance, action, and excitement that appealed to people in ways no circus could. Everyone had heard of adventures involving cowboys and Indians beyond the Mississippi River, but few people had ever been there; Cody decided he could bring the West to audiences all over the country. The following spring, Cody and a partner, a sharpshooter named Doc Carver, presented "The Wild West, Rocky Mountain and Prairie Exhibition" outdoors on the Omaha, Nebraska, fairgrounds.

After that, the Wild West Show expanded rapidly. Thousands of spectators paid 50 cents–25 cents for children–to sit in the grandstands for three hours and see the spectacle of the Old West, as Buffalo Bill unfurled it before them.

Frank and Annie decided to ask Buffalo Bill for a spot in his show. They wanted to leave the Sells Brothers' Circus, but they did not want to return to the vaudeville circuit; so many fancy shooters were cropping up on the stage that the Butlers worried their act would seem ordinary before long. They were show people, after all, and they had to make a living. Joining the Wild West troupe was the perfect opportunity for them, they decided.

Sometime during the second week of December

1884, Buffalo Bill paid a visit to the Sells Brothers' Circus in New Orleans. Hoping for the best, Frank and Annie managed to meet him. Cody was a handsome man with coal-black eyes and long hair to his shoulders; he stood so straight he seemed taller than his real height of just under six feet. Frank and Annie were probably a little nervous when they asked him outright for a job.

Cody politely said he was sorry, but he already had enough fancy shooters and had no room for the couple in his show. Annie was crushed. She didn't realize, though, that the Wild West Show included the celebrated Captain Bogardus, who was a part-owner, and that his own sons, all crack shooters, performed with him. "The knowledge of this fact put my wounded vanity 'kind of straight,'" she later wrote.

Then in March 1885, news reached the Butlers that Bogardus had quit. Annie wasted no time in writing to

> Although the Wild West Show was a popular success, Buffalo Bill Cody had some trouble hanging on to financial partners. First, Doc Carver quit midway through the first year. Then in December 1884, Cody's second partner and main sharpshooter, Captain Bogardus, decide to leave, having lost his equipment in the Mississippi steamboat collision.

Cody. She renewed her request to join his show and dared to state that she and Frank would need a high figure as their salary. Cody wrote back and said he was interested, but he had two concerns: her terms were too steep, and Bogardus had used a shotgun, not a rifle or pistol as the Butlers were accustomed to using. Cody knew that plenty of fancy shooters could knock a cork out of a bottle on stage, but using a shotgun to hit clay pigeons "on the wing"– as they skipped through the air, in other words– required more skill and stamina. Could Annie even stand the recoil of a shotgun, dozens of times a day, sometimes six days a week?

Annie countered with a no-risk offer: she and Frank would perform for three days without pay, and Annie would shoot with a shotgun. If Cody wasn't satisfied, no harm would be done. Cody agreed; he asked the Butlers to report to Louisville, Kentucky, in late April when the Wild West Show would begin a new season.

Annie didn't have much experience with shotguns, but she used the next few weeks to put herself on a grueling practice schedule. One day, she took three 16-gauge shotguns to a gun club outside Cincinnati and, over the course of nine hours, broke

4,772 glass balls out of 5,000—a new record for a man or a woman.

A few weeks later, on April 24, she and Frank arrived in Louisville for their three-day audition. When the show's manager, Nate Salsbury, saw Annie warming up, he hired her on the spot—without the three-day test and without even consulting Buffalo Bill. Later that morning, Salsbury took Annie and Frank over to meet everyone. Buffalo Bill bowed slightly as he shook her hand and called her Missy, a nickname that stuck. Then he passed Annie and her husband down the line of performers: John Nelson, who had guided Brigham Young to Utah; Buck Taylor, the six-foot-four "King of the Cowboys"; Sioux and Pawnee Indians such as White Eagle and Little Brave; and a host of other colorful people from American history. Annie remembered later, "Every head bowed before me and friendly rough hands covered mine."

Although she would be the only white woman in the show, Annie soon made clear the rules of acceptable behavior around her. None of the men cursed or drank to excess in her presence. If she met some of the men in town and they were drunk, they knew better than to speak to her. She herself never

Buffalo Bill is surrounded by Native American performers in this postcard. Cody was fairly open-minded by the standards of the day: he hired many Indians to work for him each year, and he felt that pay should be equal for women and men.

smoked, and she would only drink a beer if someone else bought it for her. On the other hand, the respect she insisted on didn't separate her from the men she performed with year after year—just the opposite, in fact. In her autobiography, Annie wrote, "A crowned queen was never treated with more reverence than was I by those wholesouled cowboys. For seventeen long years I was just their little sister, sharing both their news of joy and sorrow from home."

The start of Annie Oakley's long career with the

Wild West Show in 1885 marked a final shift in the business side of Frank and Annie's relationship. Until now, they had taken turns getting top billing on posters advertising their act. But Buffalo Bill was paying for Annie as his star, not Frank. From then on, her name alone appeared on posters as "Champion Markswoman." Frank settled down comfortably to acting as her manager and her assistant in the arena.

And she put on quite a show. At the beginning of her act, she ran into the center of the arena waving, bowing, and blowing kisses to the crowd. Then she took up her position beside a wooden table, facing a direction where no one was sitting. On the table, which was covered with a silk cloth, lay a row of shotguns and rifles—sometimes as many as 10. Frank waited nearby, his name unannounced to the crowd, preparing to load the traps and release the clay targets.

Suddenly, a single clay bird would fly out across the air, and Annie would hit it. Then a pair appeared, then three at once, and then finally what looked like a flock, as Annie fired astonishingly fast and accurately. A newspaper reporter recorded that one night her score of hitting glass balls was 55 out of 56. She could also shoot with either hand, holding pistols and firing in **tandem**, smashing targets. With a rifle, she could hit a playing card at 60 feet, then put five or six more holes in it as it fluttered to the ground. (For years afterward, free show or theater tickets with holes punched in them were known as "Annie Oakleys.") Her best-known trick shot, though, was aiming over the shoulder using a mirror or a shiny **bowie knife** to see her targets.

To make things fun, she threw a little acting into her performance. When a hard shot was coming up, she flipped her thick, luxurious hair over her shoulder and stood very still, hands on hips, thinking. If she missed, she turned to the audience and made a pouty face. As part of the act, if she missed again, she'd stamp her foot, grab Frank's hat, throw it up in the air, and shoot it. A gag that thrilled the audience was when an assistant would pretend to blunder out in front of her. She would gasp, turn away, and wipe her

For safety reasons, Annie Oakley rarely accepted when people dared her to shoot something out of their hand or off their head. Foolhardy shooters had been known to take challenges and then injure someone. In one case, a person was even killed on stage by accident.

BUFFALO BILL'S WILD WEST·
CONGRESS, ROUGH RIDERS OF THE WORLD.

MISS ANNIE OAKLEY,
THE PEERLESS LADY WING-SHOT.

This Wild West Show poster features Annie Oakley. The central drawing shows her wearing numerous shooting medals and awards, while the other images show her shattering glass balls during her show.

forehead as if she'd almost killed him. At the end of her act, Annie laid her last gun on the table, blew kisses to the audience, then ran off, pausing at the last second to give a little kick with her heel—her trademark farewell.

When the show reached Buffalo, New York, that summer of 1885, Cody added another attraction to the Wild West Show, one that left audiences awestruck: Chief Sitting Bull. The rumor was that he had agreed to travel with the show because he wanted to see Annie Oakley. Actually, Sitting Bull hoped to meet President Grover Cleveland and make a personal plea for the welfare of Indians.

On the day Sitting Bull arrived, he sat in a carriage and watched the show. Performers came over to be introduced. Annie greeted him and asked whether he had received the red silk handkerchief and the coins she had sent him. "I got them," Sitting Bull said through an interpreter, "but I left them at home for safety. I'm very glad to see you. I have not forgotten you and feel pleased that you want to remember me." Their friendship flourished. During their time together in the show, Annie taught Sitting Bull how to write.

Everywhere the Wild West Show played, audiences turned out in huge numbers to see the once-feared chief who had ordered the attack on Custer, Annie Oakley's incredible shooting act, and all the rest of the performances. In July 1886, during four weeks in New York City, 360,000 spectators—an average of 14,000 a day—paid admission to see the show. The famous writer Mark Twain suggested to Buffalo Bill that next the show should go abroad and introduce Europeans to something really American.

The following year, in 1887, the Wild West sailed for England.

This picture of Annie Oakley was taken in Glasgow, Scotland, during the Wild West Show's 1887 visit to Great Britain. Annie's charm and skill impressed European audiences as much as they did American crowds.

FAME AND FORTUNE

The Wild West Show went to England to participate in the celebration of Queen Victoria's Golden Jubilee. In April 1887, the ship *State of Nebraska* departed New York City with all the show's performers aboard. Down in the ship's hold were 18 buffaloes, 181 horses, 10 elk, four donkeys, five longhorn Texas steers, two deer, and a stagecoach.

Londoners eagerly awaited the arrival of the show. Booksellers offered copies of famous American novels about the wilderness, such as James Fenimore Cooper's *The Last of the Mohicans.* Posters featuring Indians, a runaway stagecoach, and cowboys appeared all over the city. When the ship docked on the Thames River, crowds watched in fascination as props and strange animals were unloaded, while the performers gaily disembarked to answer questions from news reporters clamoring at the bottom of the ramp. The official arrival of the Wild West Show in London would mark the start of 15 years of unbroken popularity with audiences all over Europe and the United States.

The show was slated to be part of a larger event, the American Exhibition, erected on 23 acres of gardens, courts, and exhibition halls in Earl's Court in London's West End. Londoners were already a little weary of trade shows, however, and wanted to witness the "real West."

On opening day, May 2, a throng of thousands of people listened as a choir sang "The Star-Spangled Banner" and then "Rule Britannia." But when a band struck up a rousing version of "Dixie," the crowd could contain itself no longer and stampeded past all the exhibits toward the Wild West Show. "All the world and his wife was there," a reporter for the evening news commented dryly.

The fashionable and famous flocked to the enormous grandstands; altogether, half a million people saw the show in its first three weeks. Spectators included the Irish novelist and playwright Oscar Wilde, Lady Randolph Churchill, playwright William Gilbert and composer Arthur Sullivan, the British prime minister William Gladstone, and dozens of members of aristocratic families. At the command performance held for Edward, Prince of Wales, the prince leapt up from his seat when the Indians came riding in, war-whooping, and he remained standing for most of the show.

Annie caught the eye of all London right away, as much for her frank remarks as for the contrast between her feminin-

Though Annie was popular with royalty, she never forgot her own difficult childhood. She performed special shows for orphans while visiting Europe. Also, although Frank and Annie never mentioned it, several sources say they paid for the college education of 20 orphans in the United States.

ity and her shooting skill. For example, everyone in England knew that Prince Edward was having an affair, embarrassing his wife of 24 years, Princess Alexandra. So when the prince beckoned Annie to his box, she turned instead to the princess and shook her hand first, surprising British onlookers. "You'll have to excuse me, please," Annie told the prince, "because I am an American and in America, ladies come first." Weeks later, when Buffalo Bill took the show to Windsor Castle for a command performance for the queen and her guests, the prince asked Annie if she felt intimidated about performing before royalty.

"Why, no," Annie replied honestly, "I have shot before 30,000 Americans." The prince was so astonished he just looked at her and then laughed.

The British press seemed to enjoy painting a colorful picture of Annie, adding details to her life's story that were often thrilling but untrue. "Annie Oakley is a great favorite here," reported an American who visited London during the summer of 1887. Frank, on the other hand, was so little noticed that few people knew the couple was married. Annie even received a marriage proposal from a French count who threatened suicide if she refused him. (He was "the ugliest monkey you ever saw," Annie said.) When the count sent a photograph of himself, she put a bullet through the forehead, wrote "Respectfully declined," and mailed it back. Invitations to social events, hunting outings, and shooting matches, however, she happily accepted almost daily. The prestigious London Gun Club on Notting Hill invited her to give a private exhibition; she not only won enthusiastic applause, but the club president gave her a special medal bearing an engraving of the clubhouse as a souvenir. She treasured it the most of all her awards and trophies.

Unfortunately, Buffalo Bill was growing restless at the attention being showered on the young woman who was merely one of many Wild West performers. A newspaper commented that Cody was "not the champion of his own show" and compared Annie's reputation as a crack shot with Buffalo Bill's. Although a marksman himself, Cody never claimed to be in competition with Annie. But the remark fed ill feelings that had been growing steadily between Buffalo Bill and the Butlers. Finally, at the end of the season, on October 31, the Butlers left the show, staying on in England for a while before returning to the United States.

The reason for the split may have been jealousy on Cody's part, or it may have stemmed from

Annie's spirited independence. In any case, the breakup was unfortunate for everyone involved. The following year, the Butlers appeared in variety theater, something they had wanted to avoid. Then they seemed to find their feet again when they joined Pawnee Bill's Wild West, a show that planned to go head-to-head with Buffalo Bill.

Cody knew by now that he had lost one of his main attractions, and he no doubt breathed a sigh of relief when Annie left Pawnee Bill after only a month. At the end of the year, she appeared in a play, *Deadwood Dick,* as Sunbeam, a white girl growing up with Indians. The script was written partly to show off Annie's shooting, but the play was dreadful, even though Annie's acting received favorable reviews. In January, the assistant manager stole the box office receipts and the play folded. Annie gallantly covered the show's debts and paid the actors herself.

By now, though, the tension between Buffalo Bill and the Butlers seemed to have eased. At Buffalo Bill's invitation, Annie and Frank rejoined the show in the spring of 1889, just in time to depart with the Wild West for a three-year tour of Europe, which would include stops in France, Spain, Italy,

Buffalo Bill and four Native American performers from his show sit in a gondola while touring Venice, Italy, in 1889. The European tours were wildly popular and made Annie Oakley an international star.

Belgium, the Netherlands, and Germany.

The tour was an eye-opener for Annie. In Paris, she rode the elevator to the top of the newly dedicated Eiffel Tower and marveled at the view. The French, however, knew little of American history and watched the Wild West Show rather icily until Annie performed and won them over. In Vienna, she put on a benefit for orphans. In Spain, she was distressed to see a poor woman rooting through the show's garbage for food for her family, and after

While the Wild West Show was in Germany, a famous incident occurred. After Crown Prince Wilhelm saw Annie shoot the ashes off a cigarette Frank held in his mouth, the prince asked her to shoot his cigarette. Annie  put the cigarette in his hand before she shot it. Some years later, after World War I had broken out, Americans joked bitterly that Annie should have shot the prince, not the cigarette.

that Annie gave her a basket of food every evening they were there.

The Butlers may have been growing a little tired of being so rootless, though. In 1892, after their return to the United States, they purchased a home in Nutley, New Jersey, about 13 miles south of New York City. They seemed to enjoy being settled between tours.

In 1893, "Colonel Cody"–the honorary rank was given to him by a Nebraska governor–brought the show to the Columbian Exposition in Chicago. Side by side with mammoth exhibitions of America's advances in science, engineering, and technology, Cody's show provided a background of the kind of values Americans liked to associate with their country—courage, creativity, and patriotism. The following year, a revolutionary technology created by Thomas A. Edison—the motion picture camera—captured Cody and 15 Indians on film. Annie became intrigued with how a camera might capture the flight of a bullet.

Over the next several years, the Butlers traveled gamely with the Wild West Show. Photographs of their tent speak eloquently of how they tried to keep their lives as organized and pleasant as possible. The wood floor of the tent was covered with a patterned rug, and Annie hung favorite pictures above small pieces of furniture. In one photograph, she is sitting in a rocking chair reading. Beside her is a woman's bicycle and near the tent is a flower garden, a favorite hobby of hers.

By the early 1900s, however, a series of events persuaded the Butlers that the best years of performing were probably behind them.

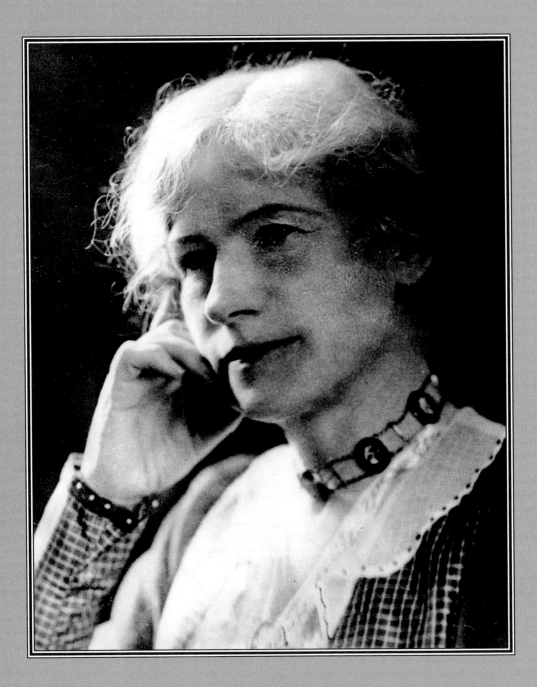

A studio portrait of Annie Oakley, taken sometime after 1902. She is wearing a necklace given to her by King Ludwig II of Bavaria. After Annie's death in 1926, a local newspaper wrote, "In the years to come, her grave will be a shrine for those who loved this woman, before whom kings and rulers of the world bowed and paid tribute, and whom all honored."

HOME TO OHIO

The Wild West Show traveled to its shows by train. On October 29, 1901, a collision with another train killed or fatally injured the animals that filled five stock cars. One man was killed. Annie was injured, but sources disagree on how severely. The Butlers reported that Annie's hip was torn, and that within 17 hours, her hair had turned snow white. Some biographers write that as a result of the accident, she had five operations on her back over the years. The matter of her hair turning white—when and why—is disputed.

Soon after the accident, Annie visited Hot Springs, Arkansas. While sitting in a steaming bath, she fainted and remained too long in the mineral water. One possibility is that overexposure to the minerals bleached her hair and left brown blotches on her skin. The Butlers may have relied on the train accident as a convenient explanation.

In any case, Annie was now in her forties. Her white hair made her appear distinguished, like a "kindly school teacher," one newspaper remarked. Frank and Annie decided it was time to retire. Annie told the press she was tired.

They moved back to their home in Nutley, New Jersey, where Annie accepted a part in another theater production about the Old West that received flattering reviews. But then, on August 11, 1903, an erroneous newspaper report created a heartache that occupied her in court for the next five years.

Two Chicago newspapers mistakenly reported that Annie Oakley had been arrested stealing money to buy cocaine. (Actually the woman arrested was a vaudeville Oakley imitator down on her luck.) Major newspapers picked up the story all over the country. Annie's shame and anger could not be erased, not even when public apologies were printed in the newspapers. She insisted on suing every one of them. For five years she took the stand in courtrooms in Chicago, St. Louis, New York, and half a dozen other places, demanding financial awards to make good on the damage done to her reputation. William Randolph Hearst, owner of several of the newspapers, sent a detective to Darke County, her birthplace, to dig up information that would discredit her. Nevertheless, she won across the board, though the settlements were far less than what she expected. Frank told the press that after paying expenses and the lawyers, practically nothing was left.

Happier times lay ahead, however, when the couple bought property and built a home in Cambridge, Maryland, in 1912.

Annie wrote her first autobiography, *Powders I Have Used,*

Frank described Cambridge as a town with "four banks, several fine churches, but no saloons." Annie worked with the builders to make sure closets and kitchen work areas were just right for a woman five feet tall. The Butlers' home is now on the Register of Historic Places.

while in Cambridge. The book was published in 1914 by a gunpowder manufacturer. She also wrote articles about shooting and hunting, and she encouraged other women to take up shooting, if only for self-defense.

During 1915 and 1916, the Butlers traveled between Cambridge; Pinehurst, North Carolina; and Newcastle-by-the-Sea, New Hampshire. The latter was a small resort owned by the owner of their hotel in Pinehurst. In 1917, the Butlers sold their home in Cambridge and moved to Pinehurst. That same year, Buffalo Bill Cody died. Annie Oakley wrote a long *eulogy* for him and for the passing of the Wild West era.

Buffalo Bill Cody's final curtain came in 1917; he died on January 10 of that year. Annie wrote about her former boss and the end of the Wild West era.

When the United States was pulled into World War I, Annie offered to raise a regiment of woman volunteers to fight. She had made the same offer during the Spanish-American War. Both times the government turned her down. At their own expense, however, Frank and Annie gave marksmanship instruction to soldiers. Annie also traveled across the country for the National War Council of the Young Men's Christian Association and the War Camp Community Service. At stops at training camps, she gave shooting demonstrations to raise money for the Red Cross.

At the end of 1922, Annie was contemplating a comeback–a whole new generation of admirers wanted to see her perform. But then she and Frank were severely injured in an automobile accident. Annie took more than a year to recover from her injuries and walked with the aid of a brace. She and Frank moved to her hometown in Ohio so that they could be near her family.

On November 3, 1926, Annie died. Eighteen days later, Frank, her husband of 40 years, died at the home of one of Annie's nieces in Detroit, Michigan. The two are buried in a small cemetery just south of Brock, Ohio.

Chronology

1860   Phoebe Ann Moses (Annie Oakley) is born on August 13 in a cabin in Darke County, Ohio

1882   Annie marries Frank Butler, a sharpshooter she defeated in a shooting contest

1884   Annie meets Chief Sitting Bull on March 20; the chief "adopts" her as his stepdaughter and nicknames her "Little Sure Shot"

1885   On April 24, Annie Oakley auditions for Buffalo Bill's Wild West Show and is hired on the spot

1887   The Wild West Show sails for England in April; Annie performs before royalty and to sellout crowds in London; the Butlers leave the Wild West Show on October 31

1889   The Butlers rejoin the Wild West Show and begin a three-year tour of Europe

1892   The Butlers purchase a home in Nutley, New Jersey

1893   The Wild West Show participates in the Columbian Exposition held in Chicago

1901   Annie is injured in a train wreck on October 29; later that year, the Butlers retire from the Wild West Show

1903   On August 11, several newspapers mistakenly report that Annie Oakley was arrested for stealing; she launches a five-year battle in the courts to clear her name

1912   The Butlers build a home in Cambridge, Maryland

1914   Annie's autobiography, *Powders I Have Used,* is published

1917   Buffalo Bill Cody dies on January 10, and Annie writes a long eulogy for him; the Butlers build a new home in Pinehurst, North Carolina

1918   Annie and Frank participate extensively in supporting America's role in World War I, often at their own expense

1922   The Butlers are severely injured in a car accident

1926   Annie dies in Greenville, Ohio, on November 3; Frank Butler dies at the home of relatives in Detroit, Michigan, on November 21

GLOSSARY

audition–a trial performance used to determine an entertainer's merits.

autobiography–the story of a person's life, as told by that person.

bowie knife–a single-edged hunting knife with part of the back edge curved to a point and sharpened.

buckshot–small lead shot that scatters when fired.

debut–a first performance before the public.

emigrate–to leave one's place of residence or country to live somewhere else.

eulogy–a formal speech praising someone, usually after the person's death.

grandstands–a roofed stand for spectators at a stadium or arena.

intriguing–fascinating; engaging the interest to a high degree.

kaleidoscope–a constantly changing pattern or scene.

marksmanship–skill in shooting at a mark or target.

mortgage–a loan for property.

notorious–widely and unfavorably known; famous in a negative sense.

pneumonia–a disease of the lungs caused by infection.

poor farm–a facility maintained at public expense for the support and employment of needy persons.

recoil–the backwards kick of a gun after it is fired.

repertoire–a list of acts a person is prepared to perform.

reservations–tracts of public land set aside for American Indians.

tandem–when two or more things are arranged one right after the other.

vaudeville–a popular form of stage entertainment during the 19th century that featured various acts, such as acrobats, performing animals, comedians, dancers, singers, and trick shooters.

winsome–pleasing and engaging because of a childlike charm and innocence.

FURTHER READING

Dadey, Debbie. *Shooting Star: Annie Oakley, the Legend.* New York: Walker, 1999.

Flynn, Jean. *Annie Oakley: Legendary Sharpshooter.* Berkeley Heights, N.J.: Enslow, 1998.

Gleiter, Jan. *Annie Oakley.* New York: Raintree, 1995.

Hamilton, John. *Annie Oakley.* Edwina, Minn.: Abdo, 1996.

Kasper, Shirl. *Annie Oakley.* Norman: University of Oklahoma Press, 1992.

Klass, Sheila Soloman. *A Shooting Star.* New York: Holiday House, 1996.

Riley, Glenda. *The Life and Legacy of Annie Oakley.* Norman: University of Oklahoma Press, 2000.

Sayers, Isabelle S. *Annie Oakley and Buffalo Bill's Wild West.* Mineola, N.Y.: Dover, 1989.

Wilson, Ellen. *Annie Oakley: Young Markswoman.* New York: Aladdin, 1989.

PICTURE CREDITS

CHARLES J. SHIELDS was chairman of the English department at Homewood-Flossmoor High School in Flossmoor, Illinois. Now he writes books and textbooks for young people. His wife, Guadalupe, is an elementary school principal in Chicago.